UNICORN

COLORING BOOKS FOR GIRLS

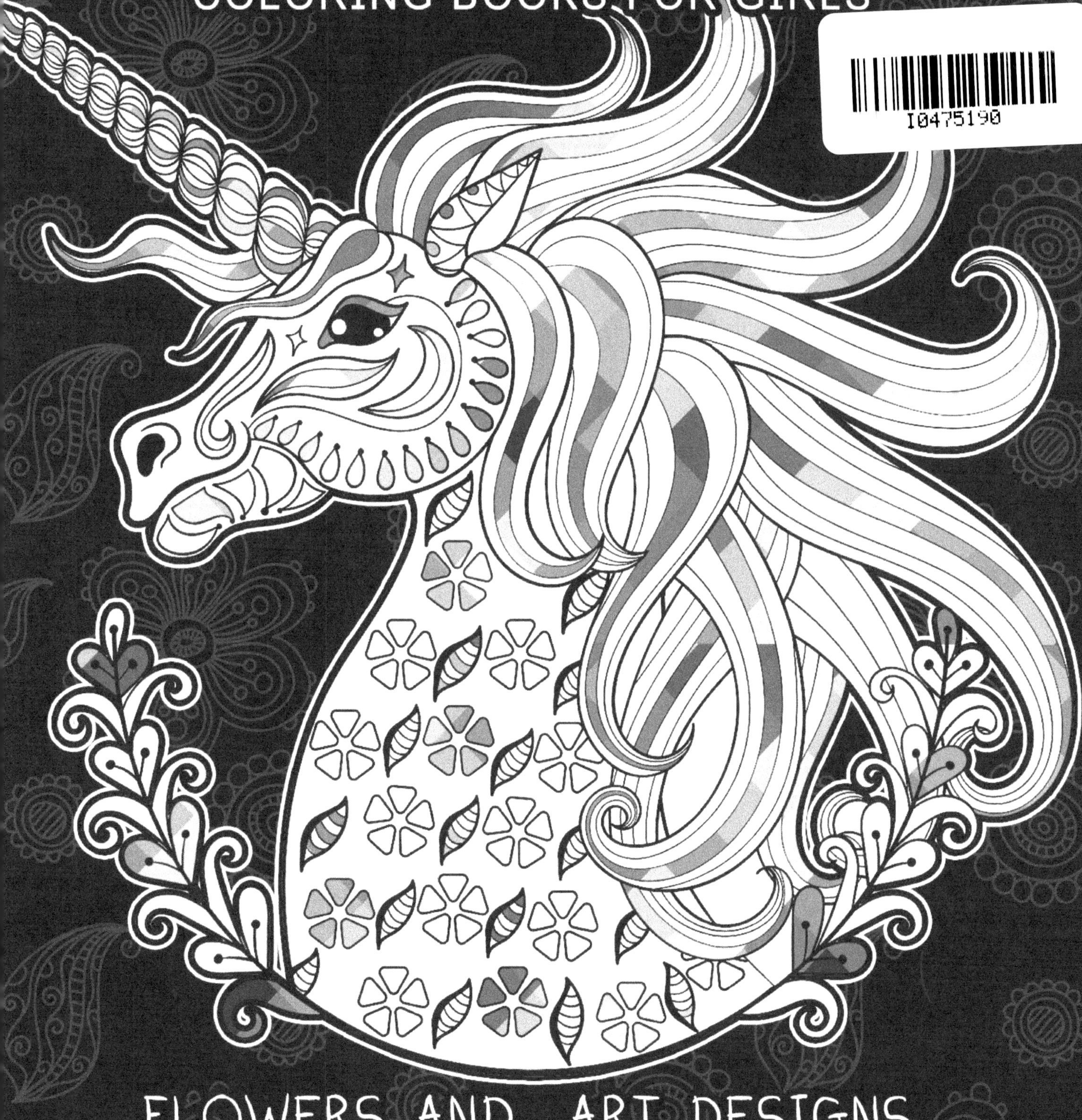

FLOWERS AND ART DESIGNS

TEST YOUR COLOR

TEST YOUR COLOR

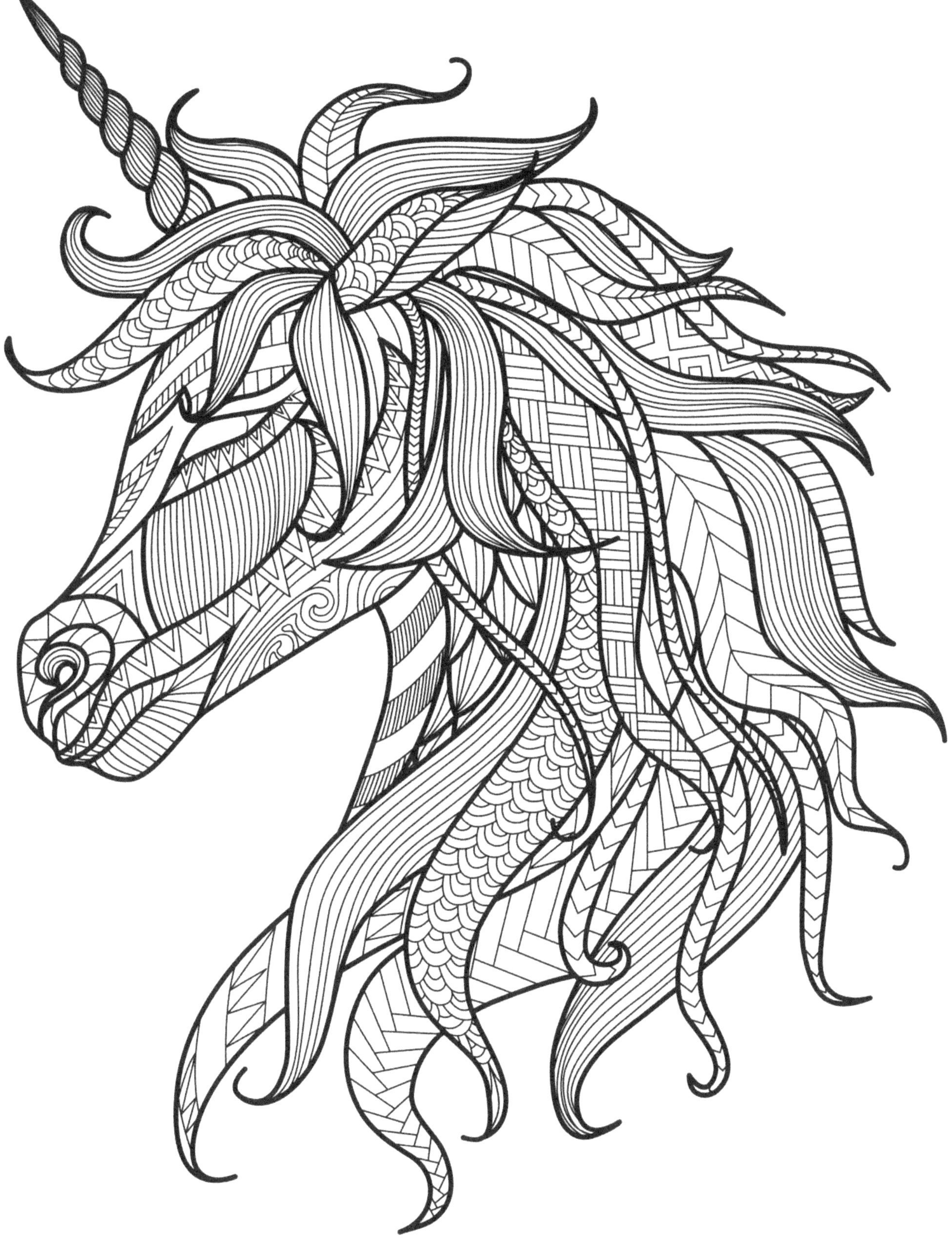

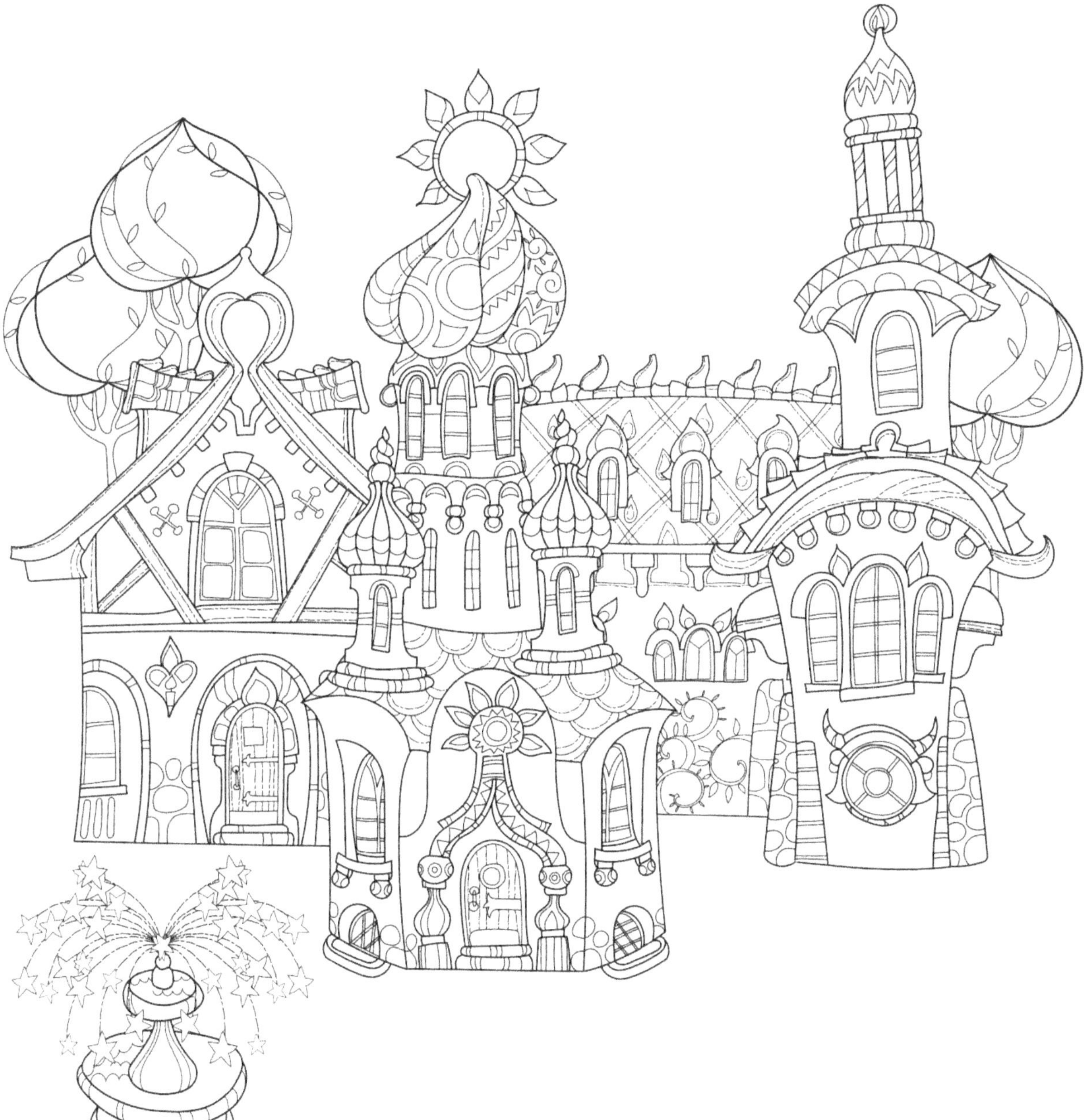

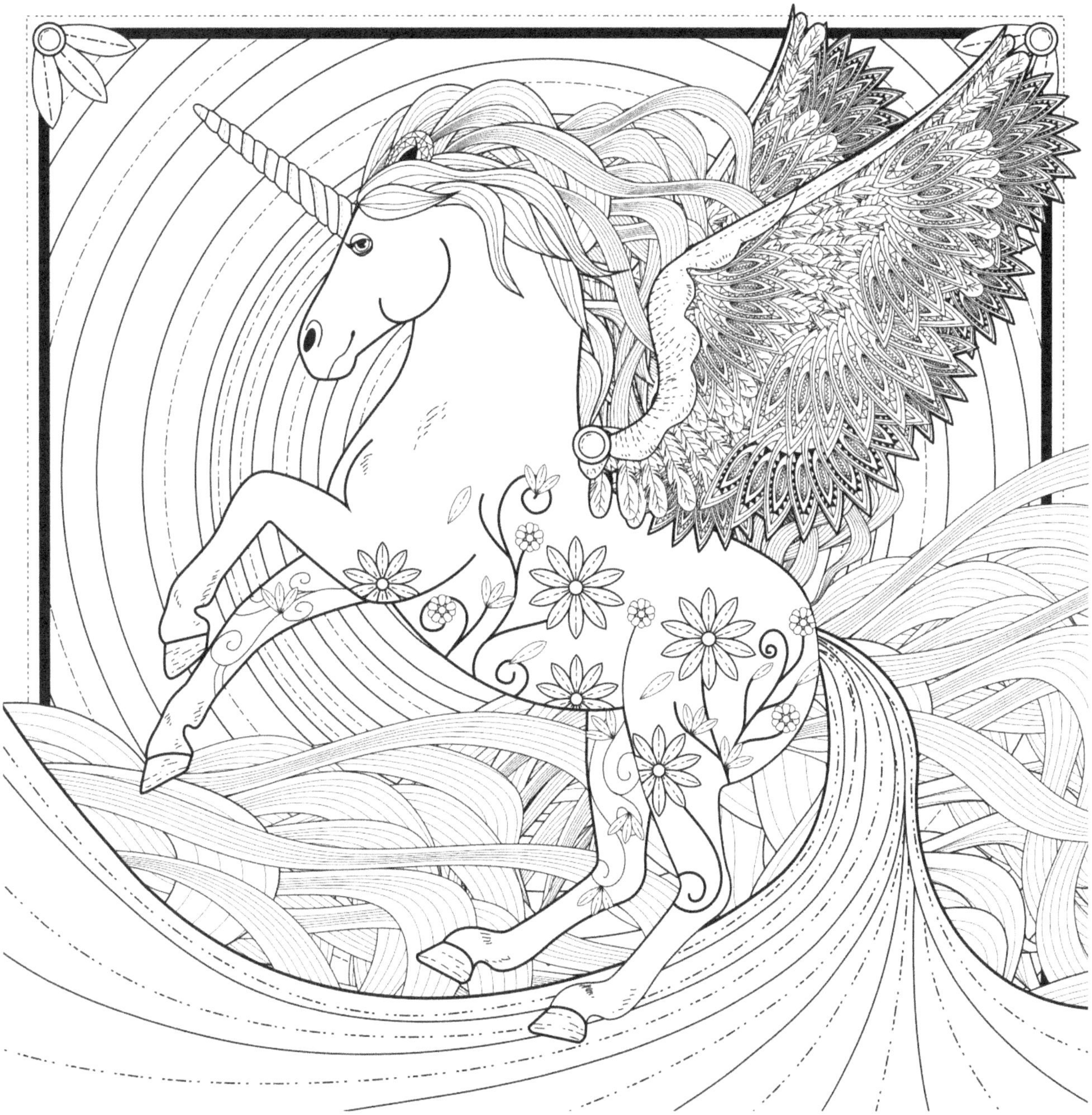

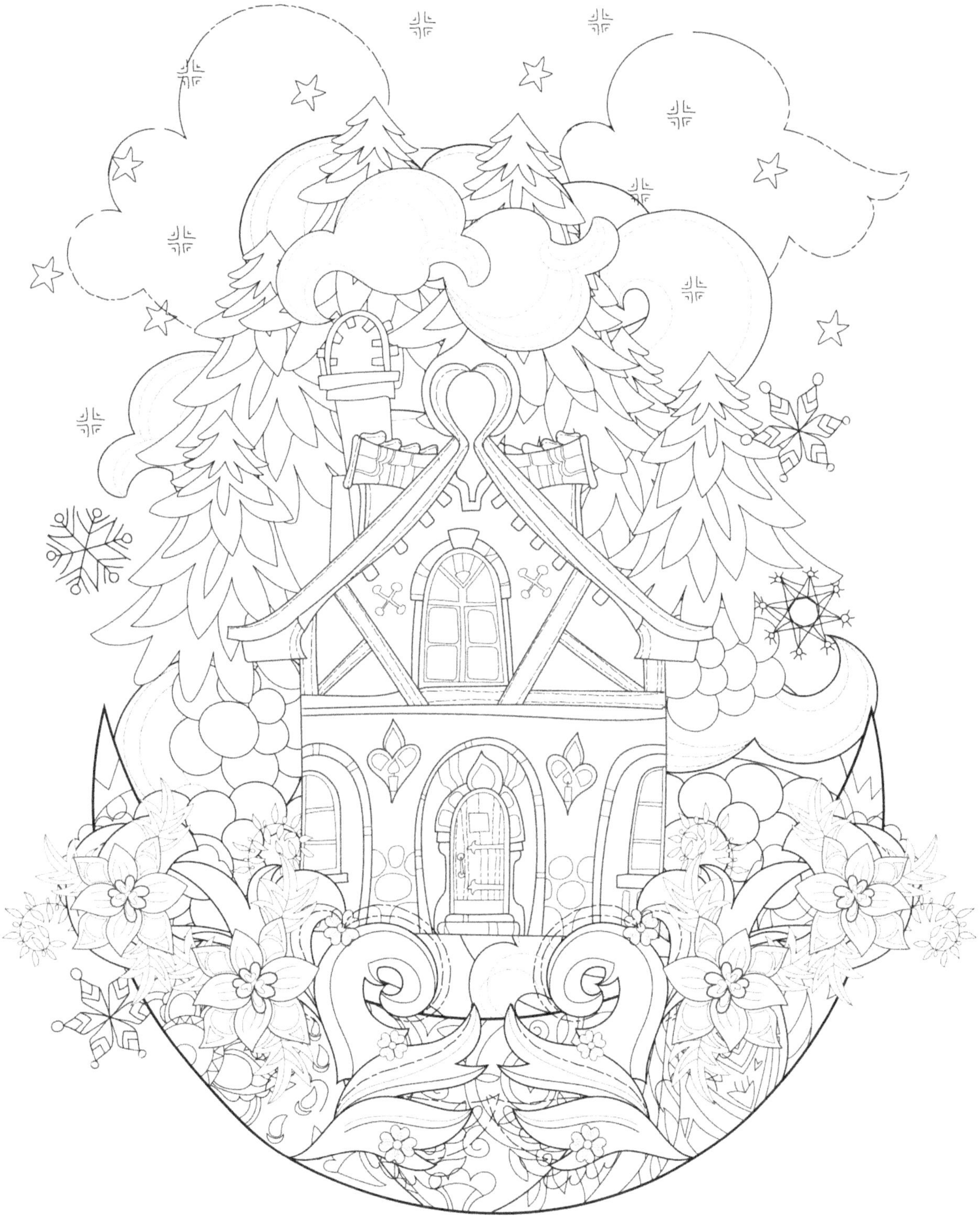

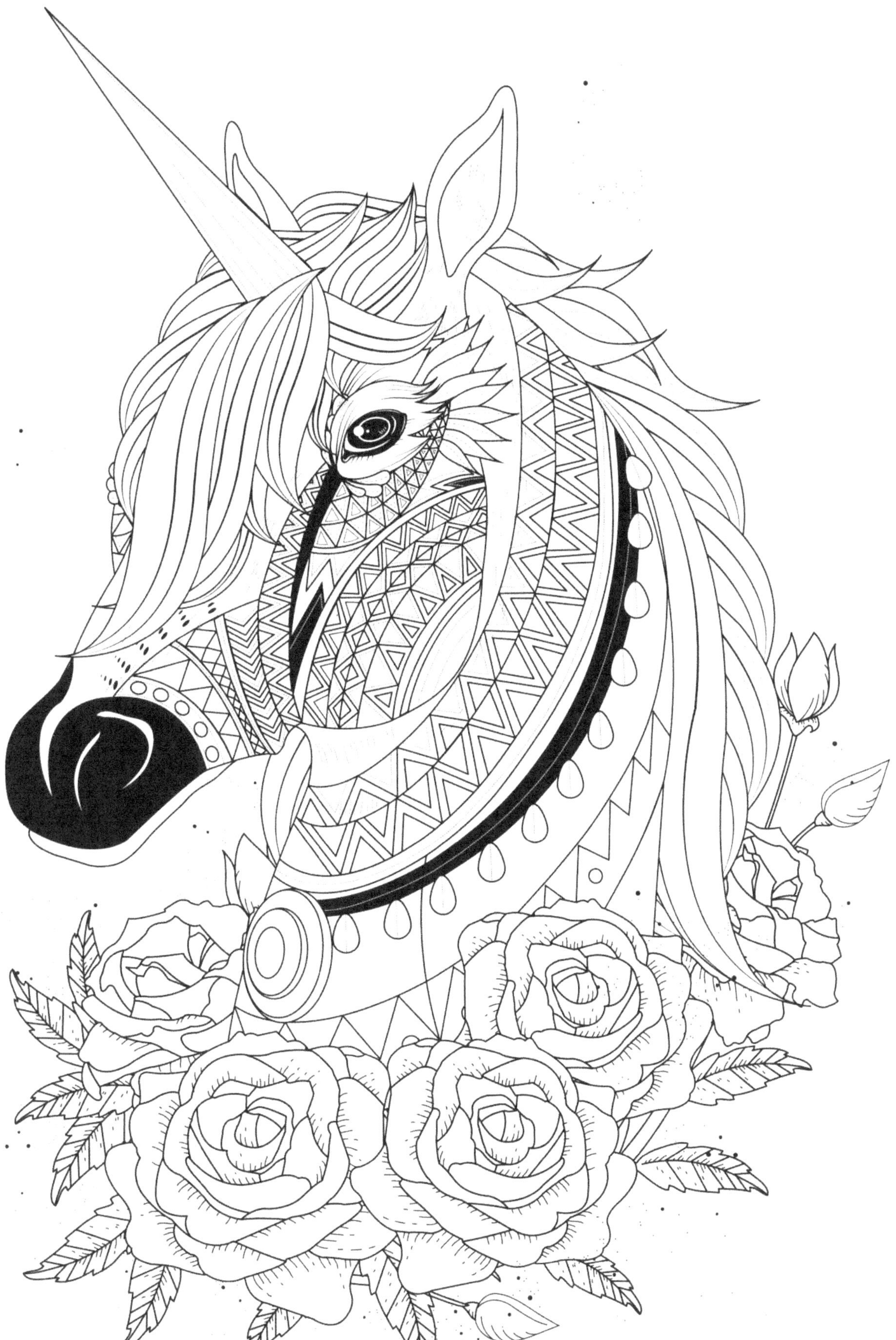

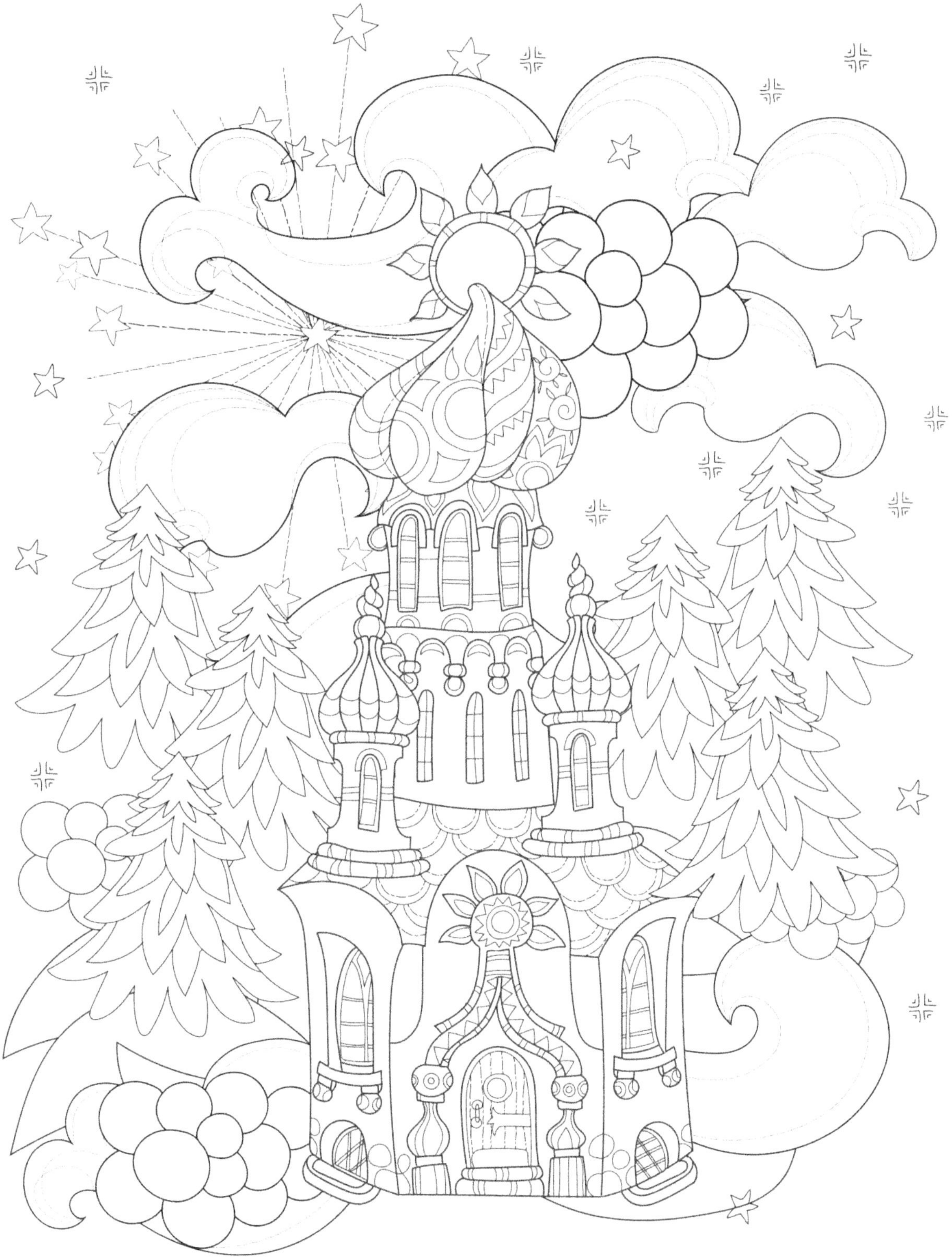

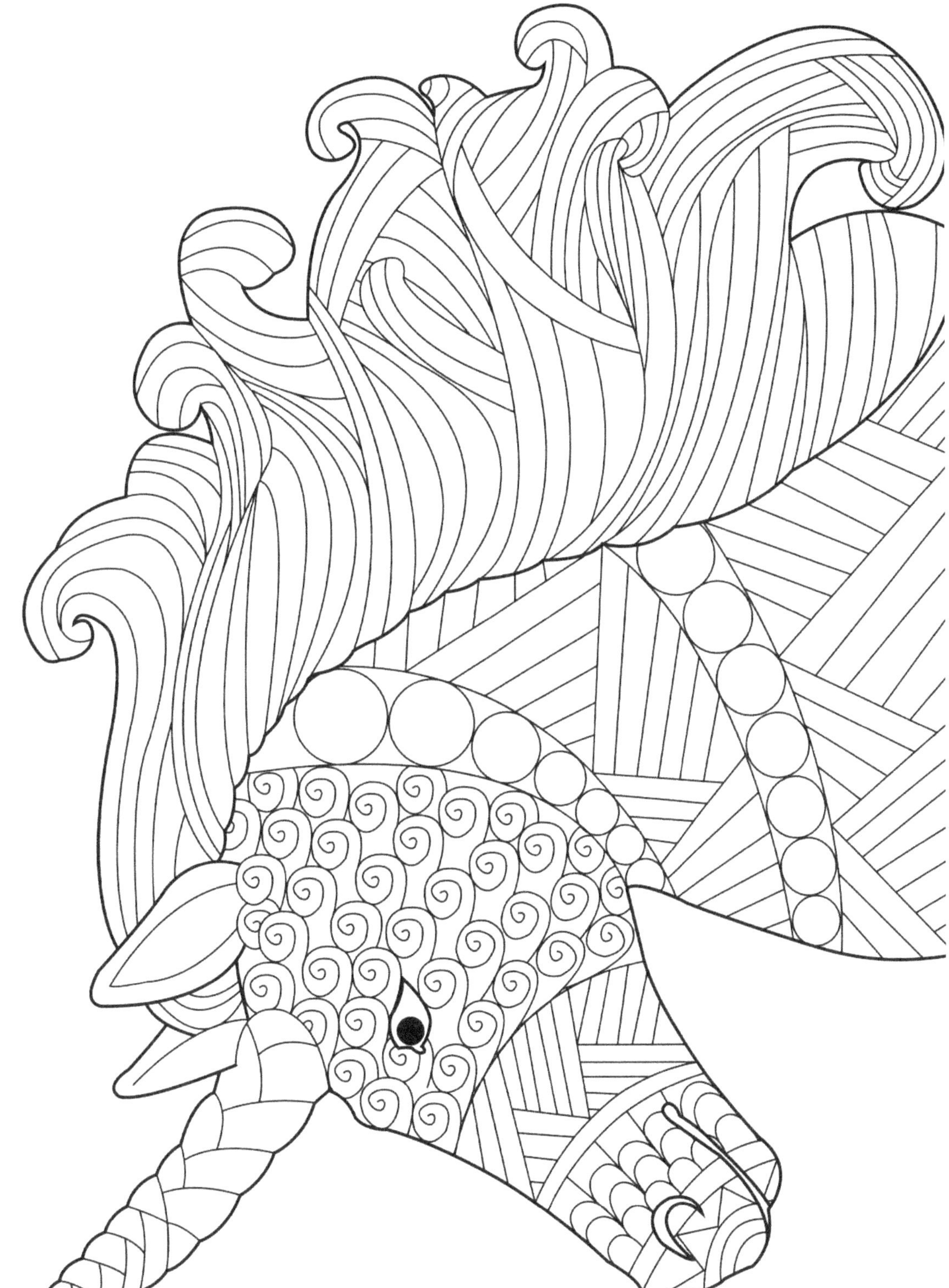

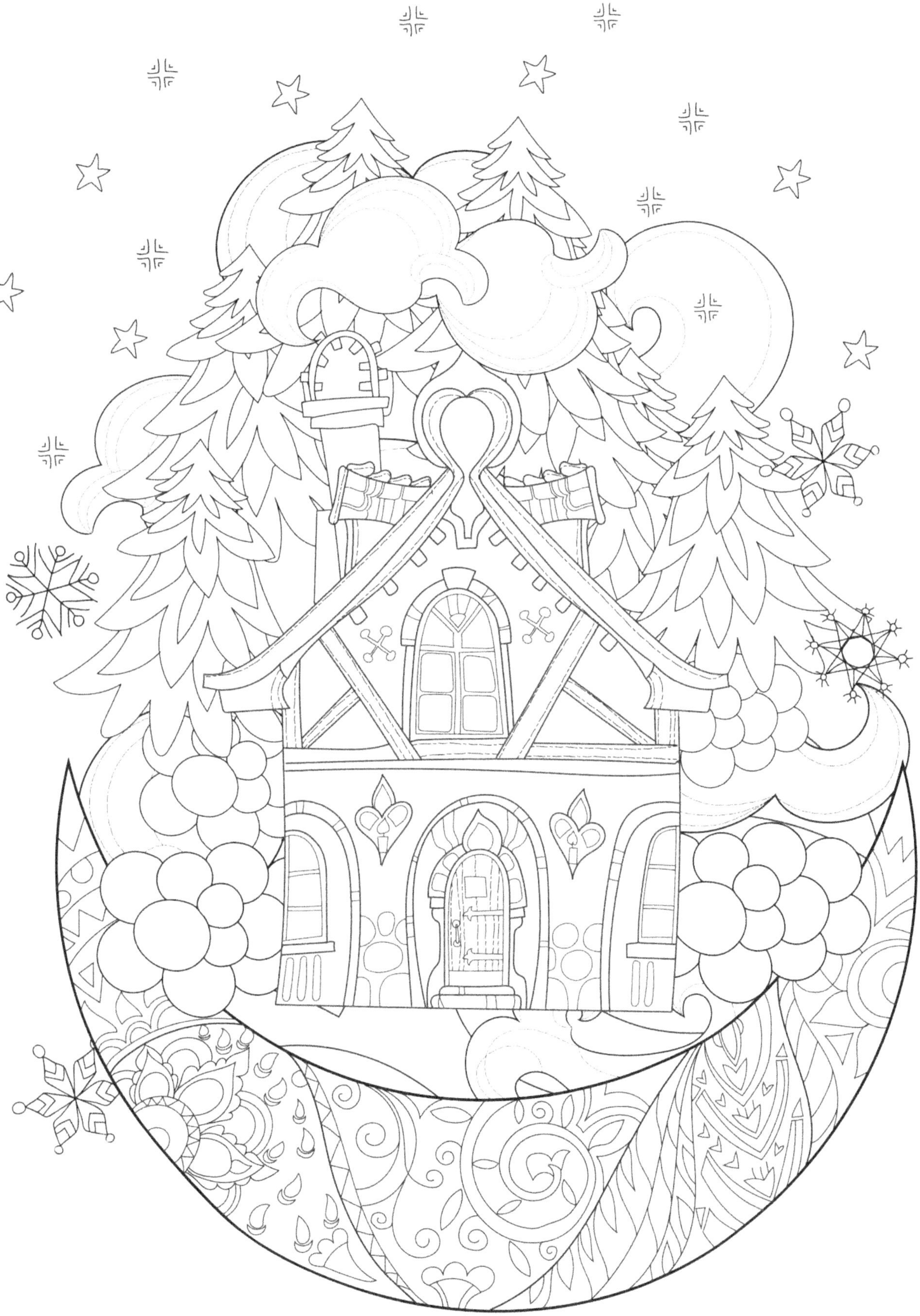

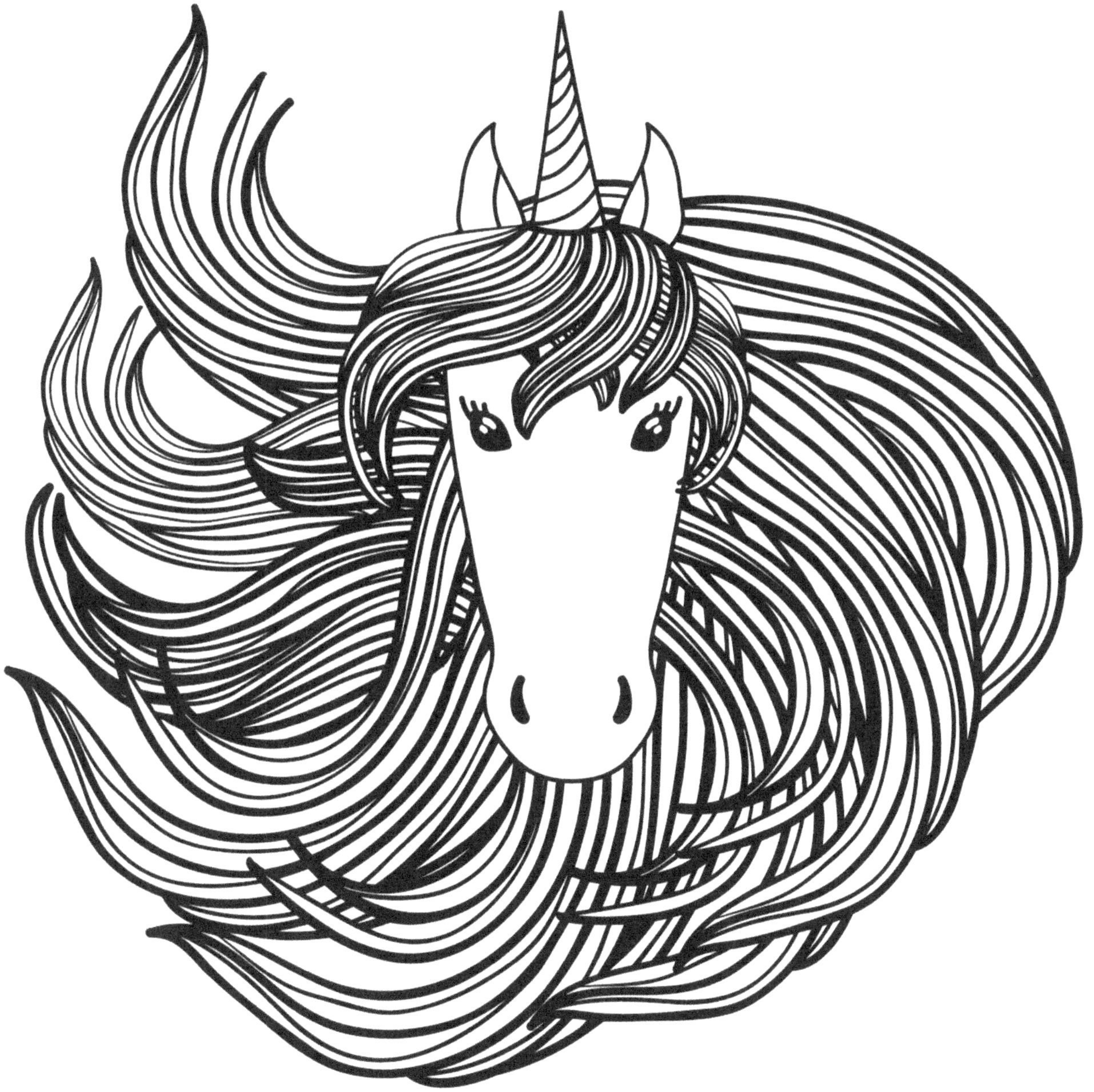

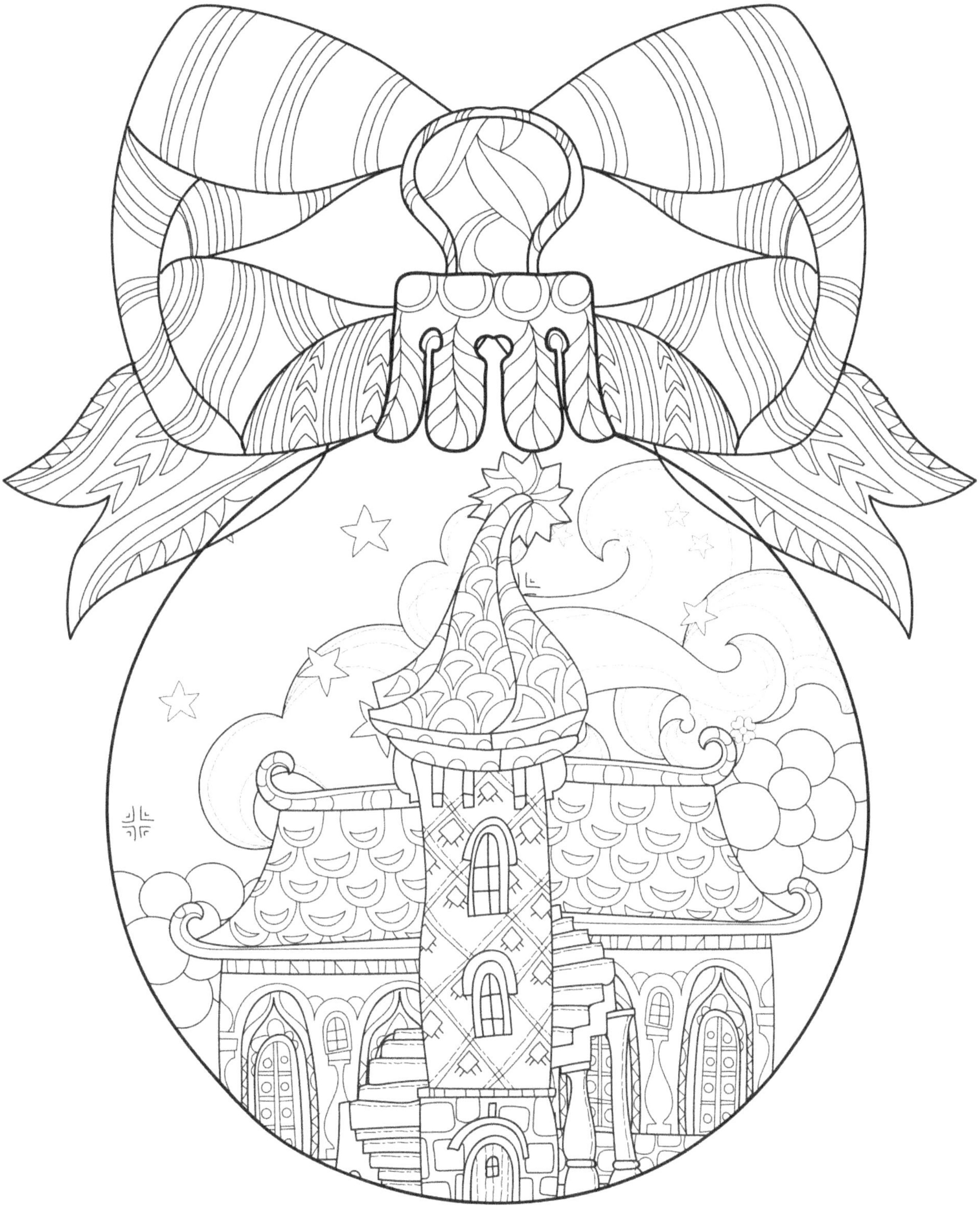

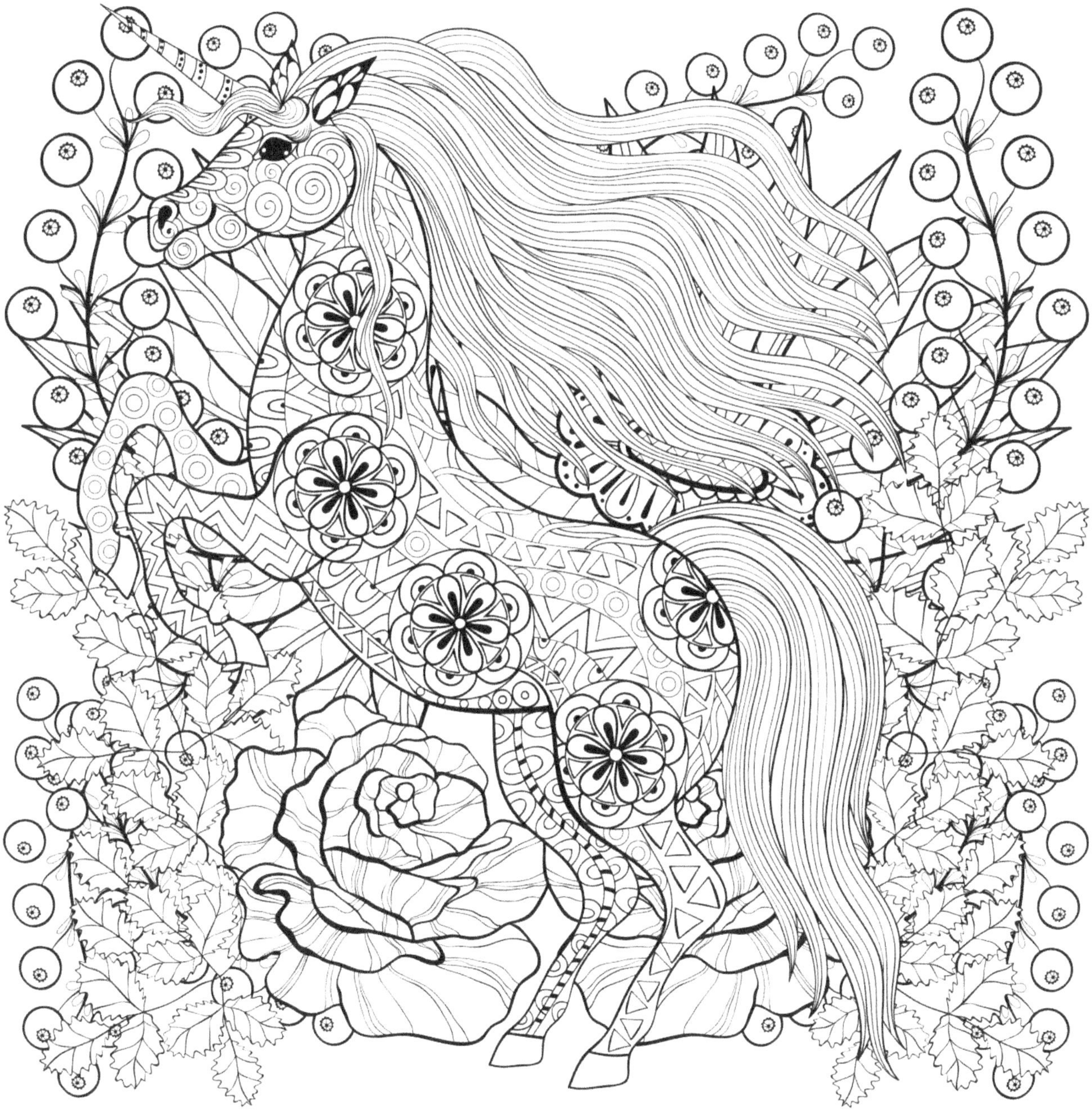

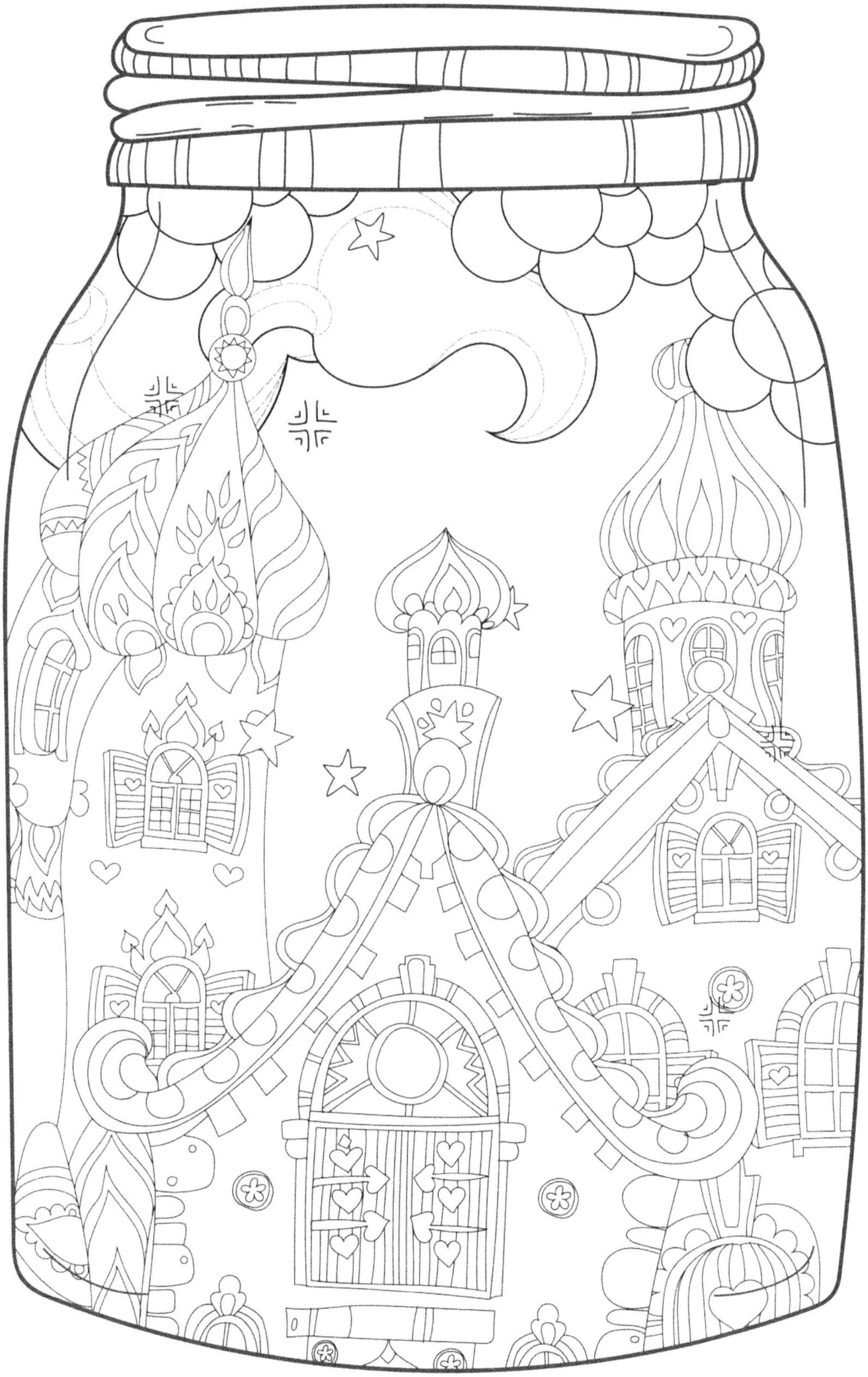

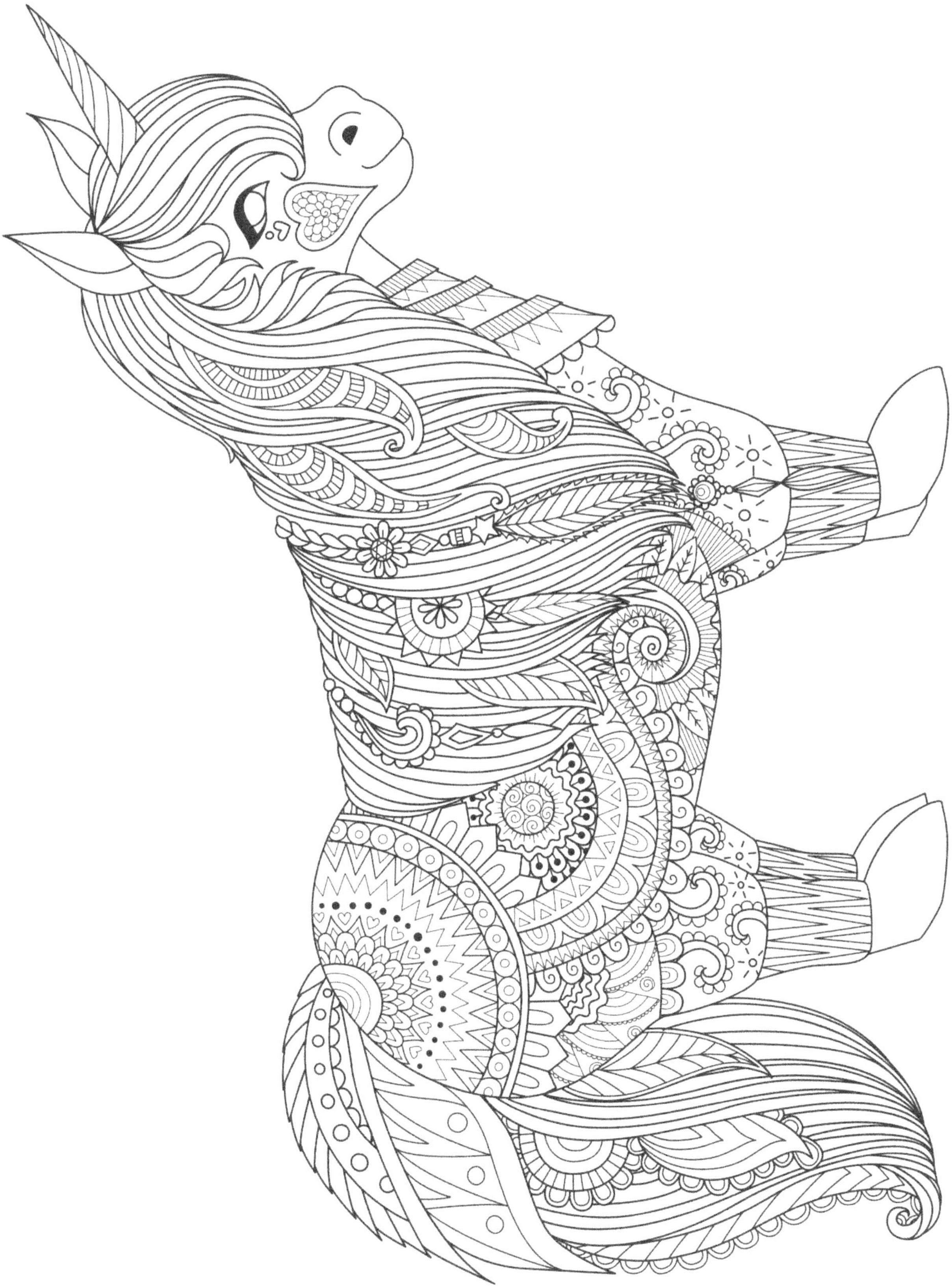

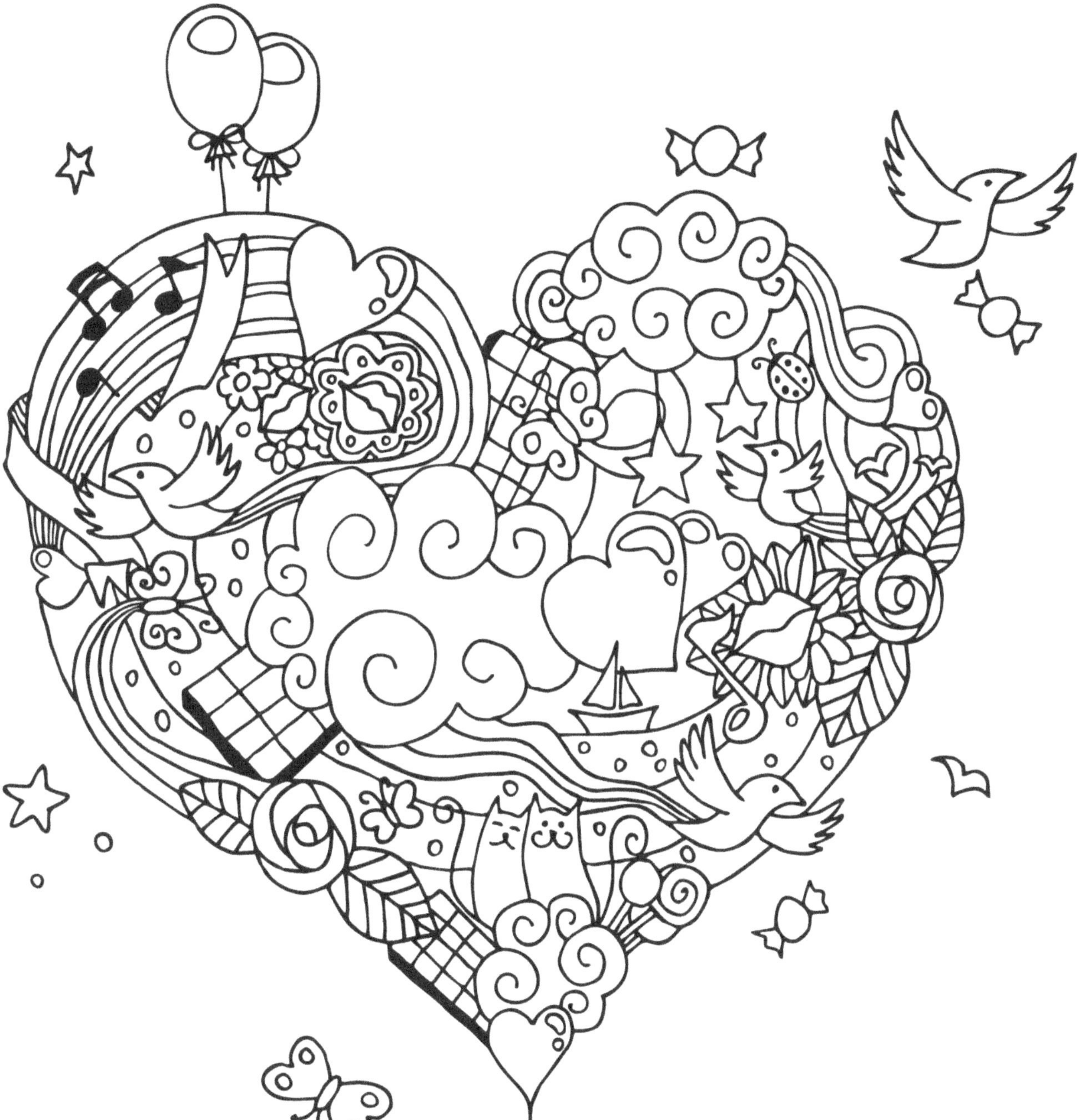

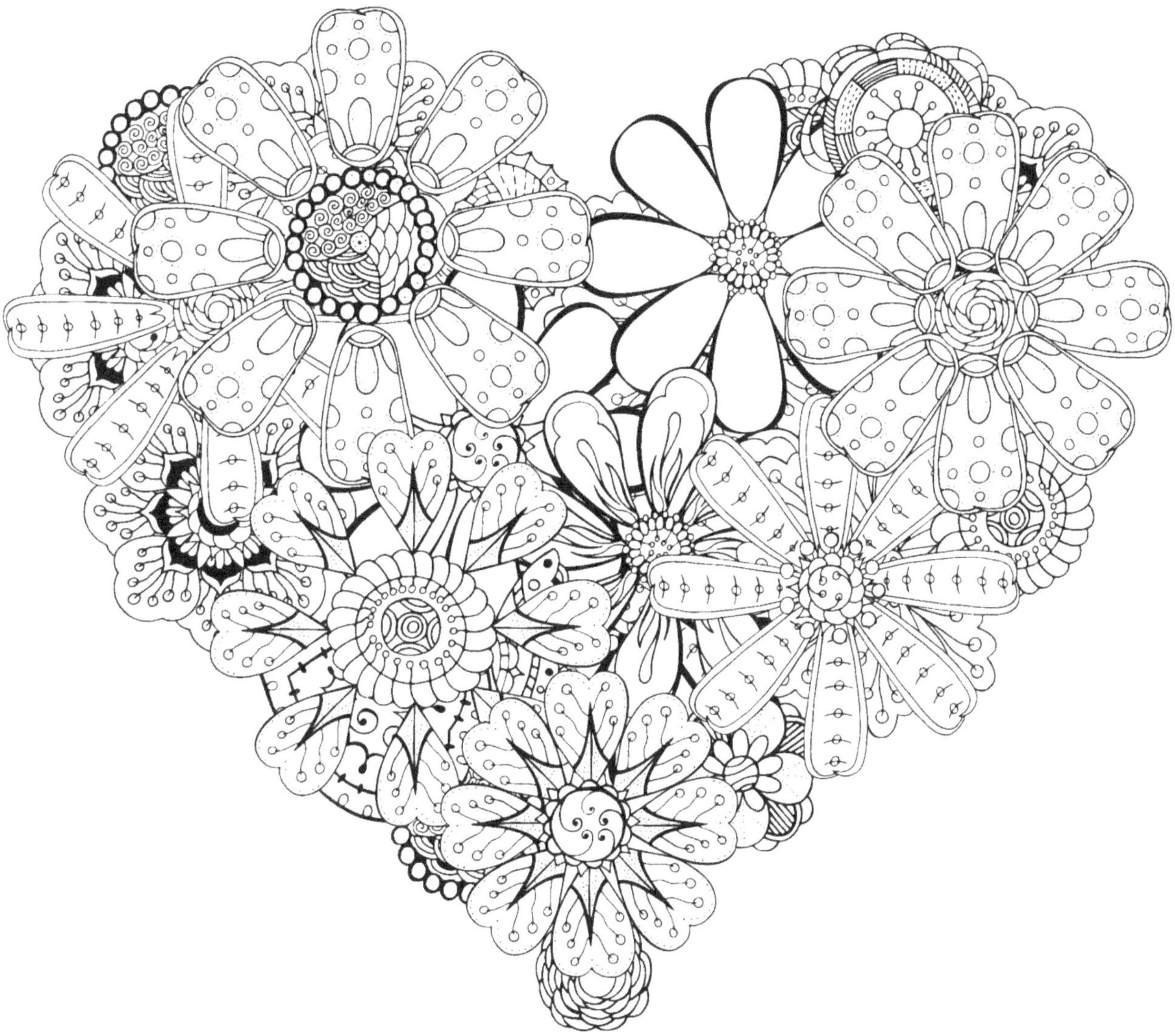

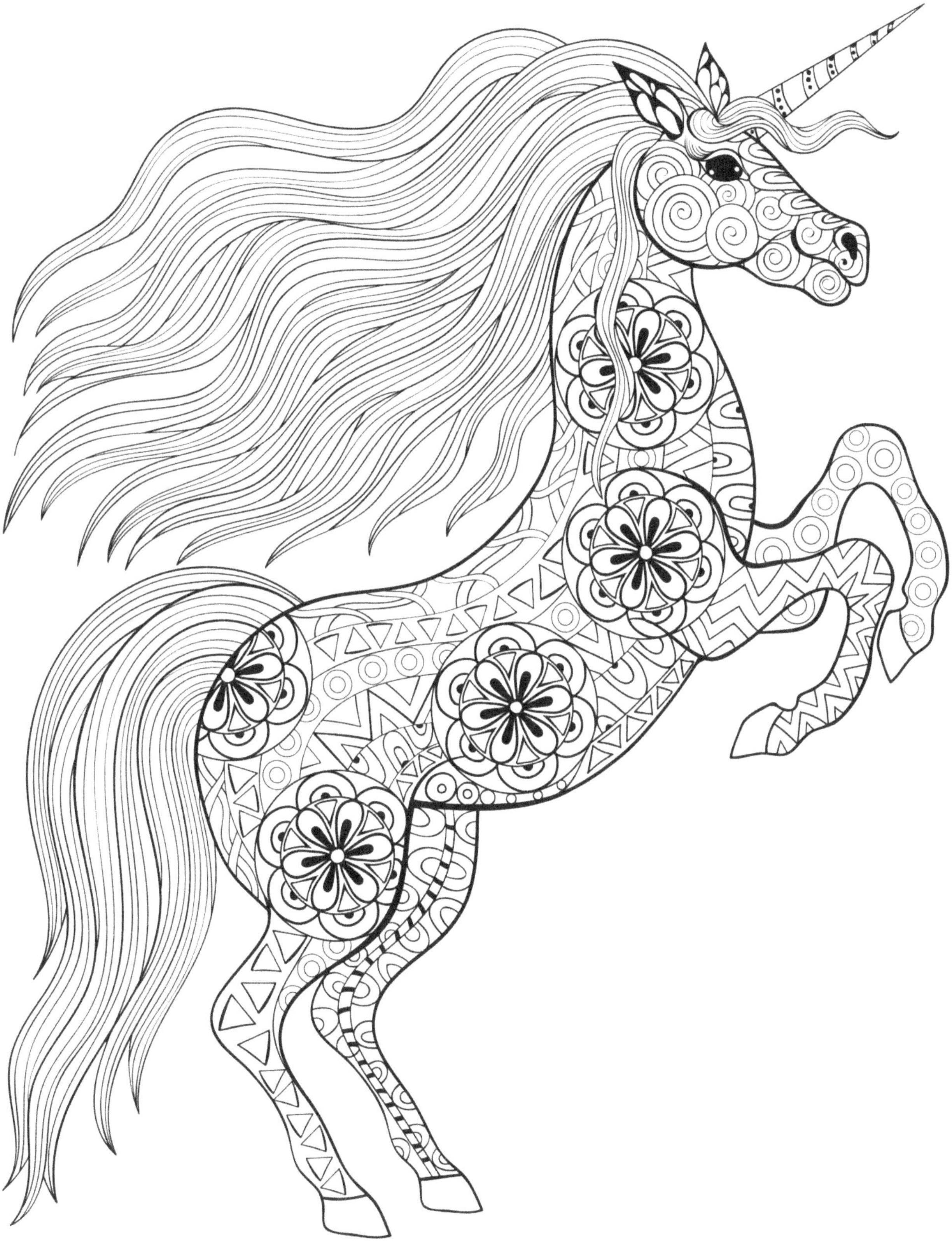

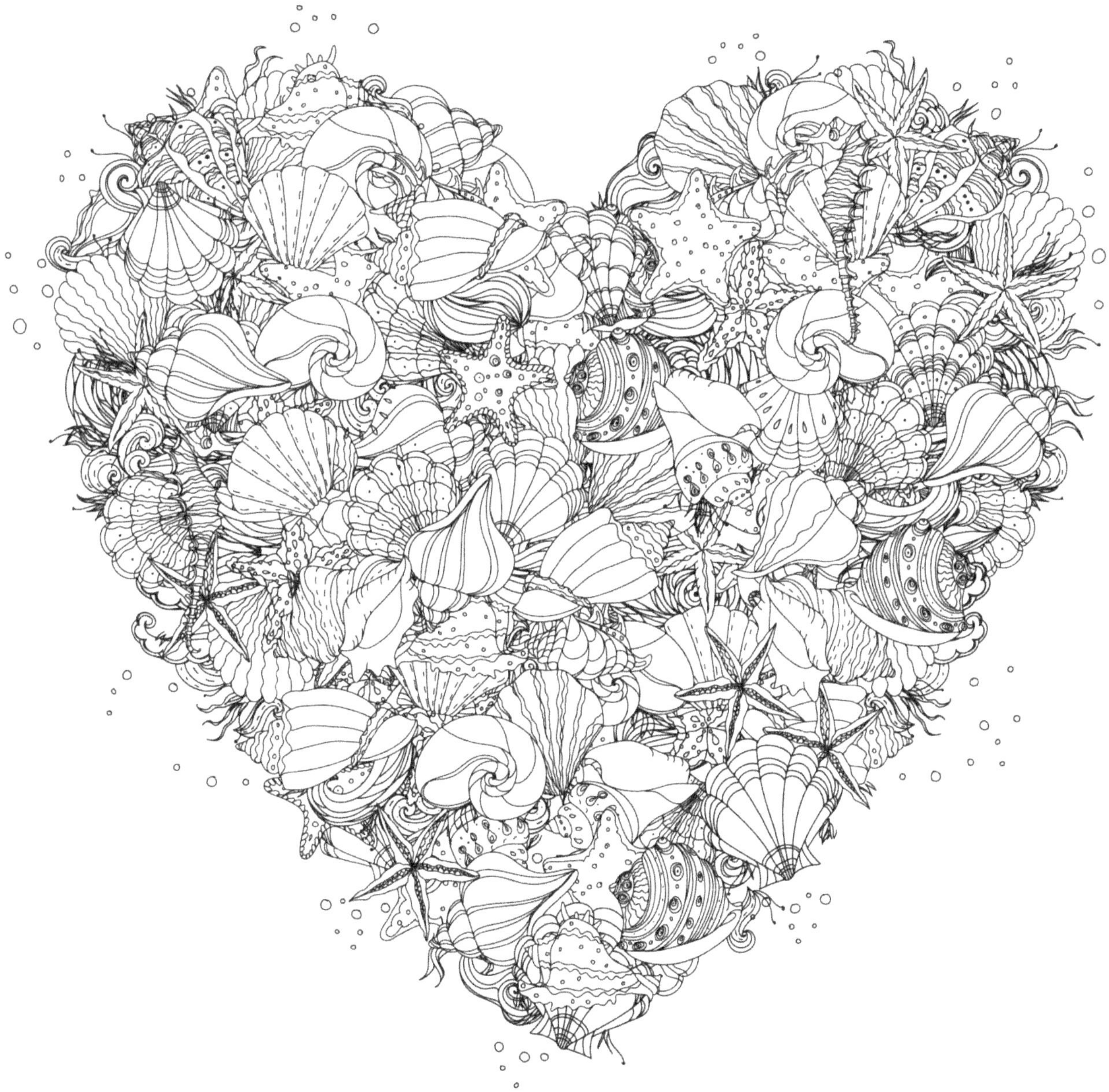

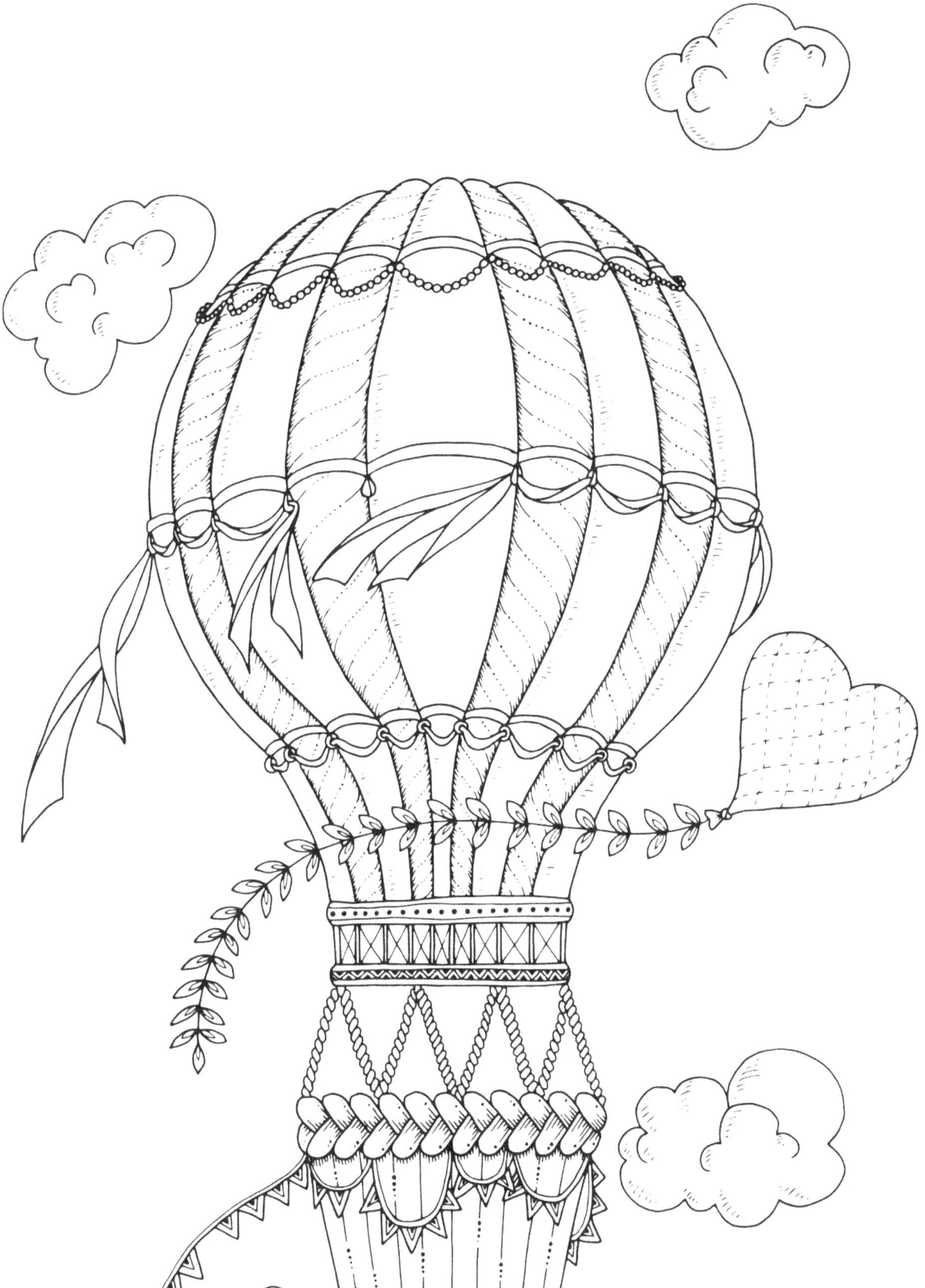

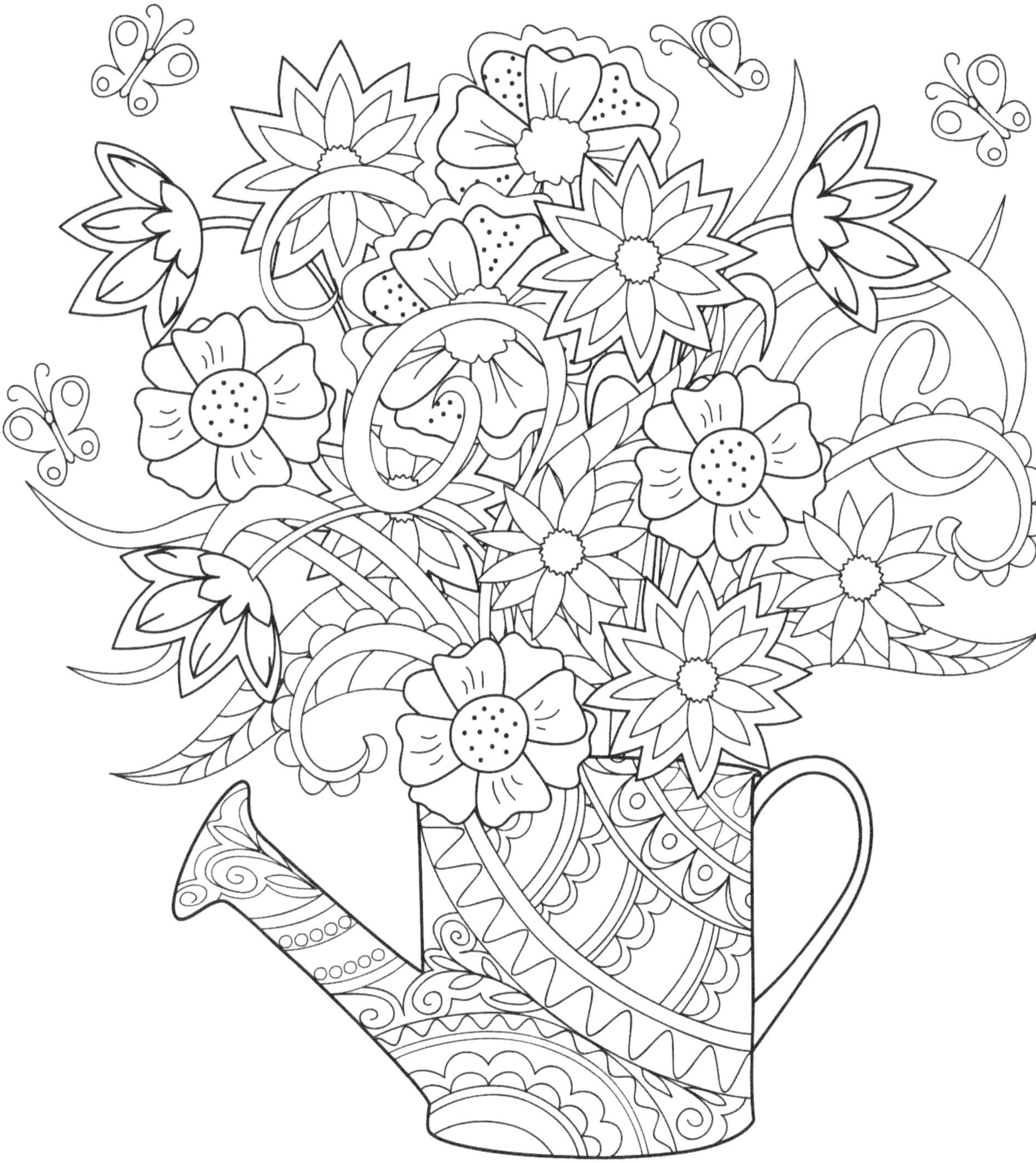

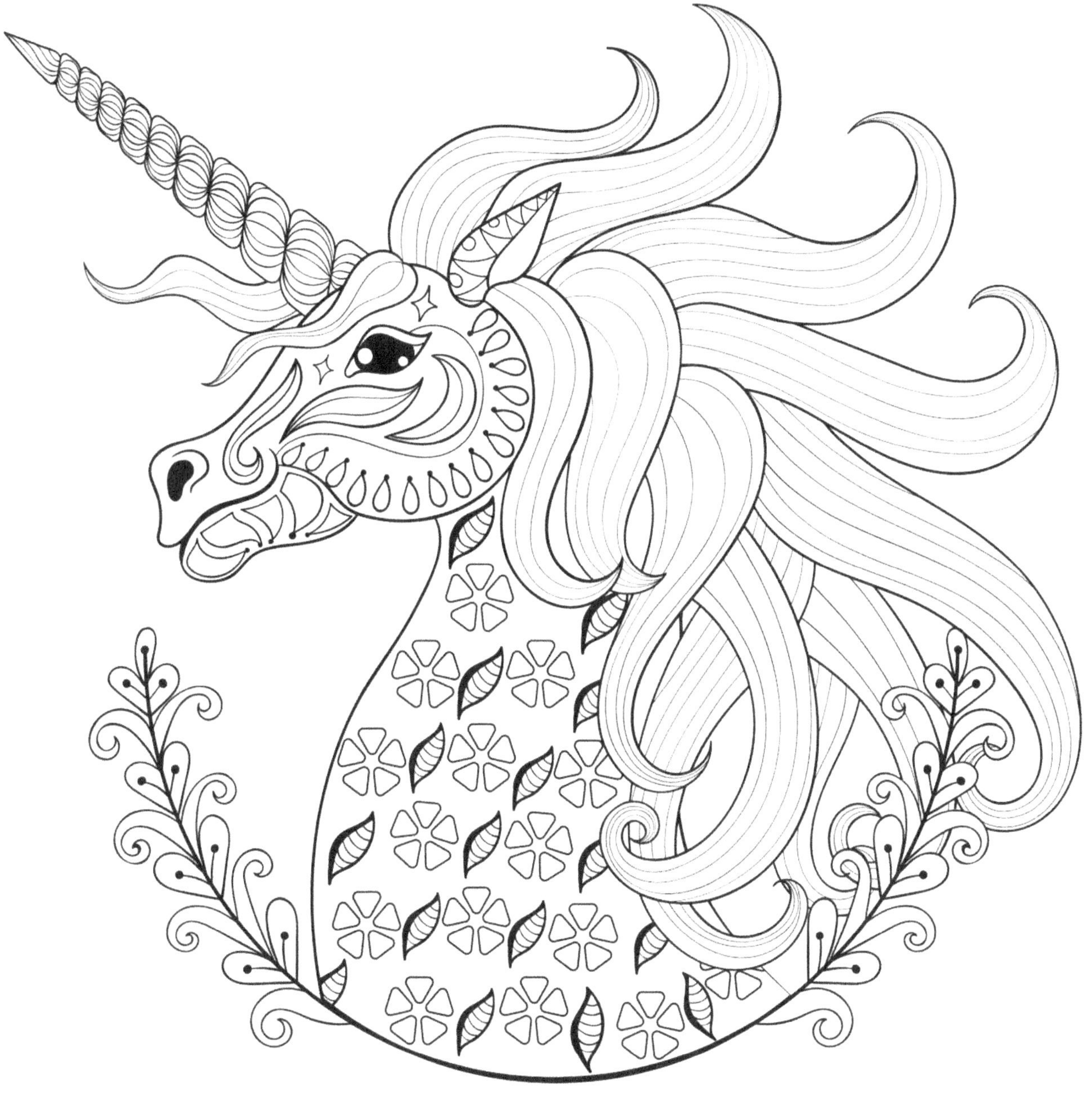

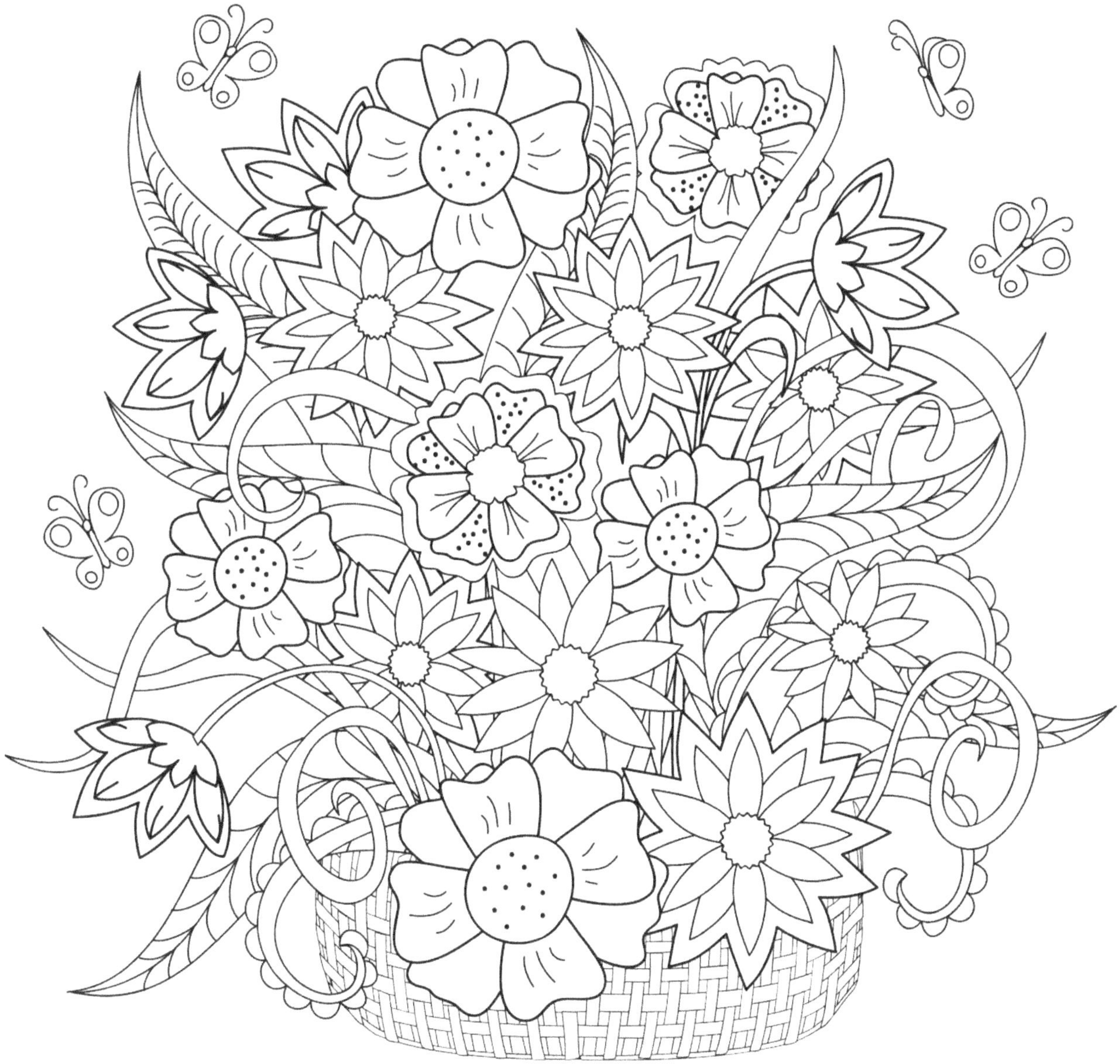

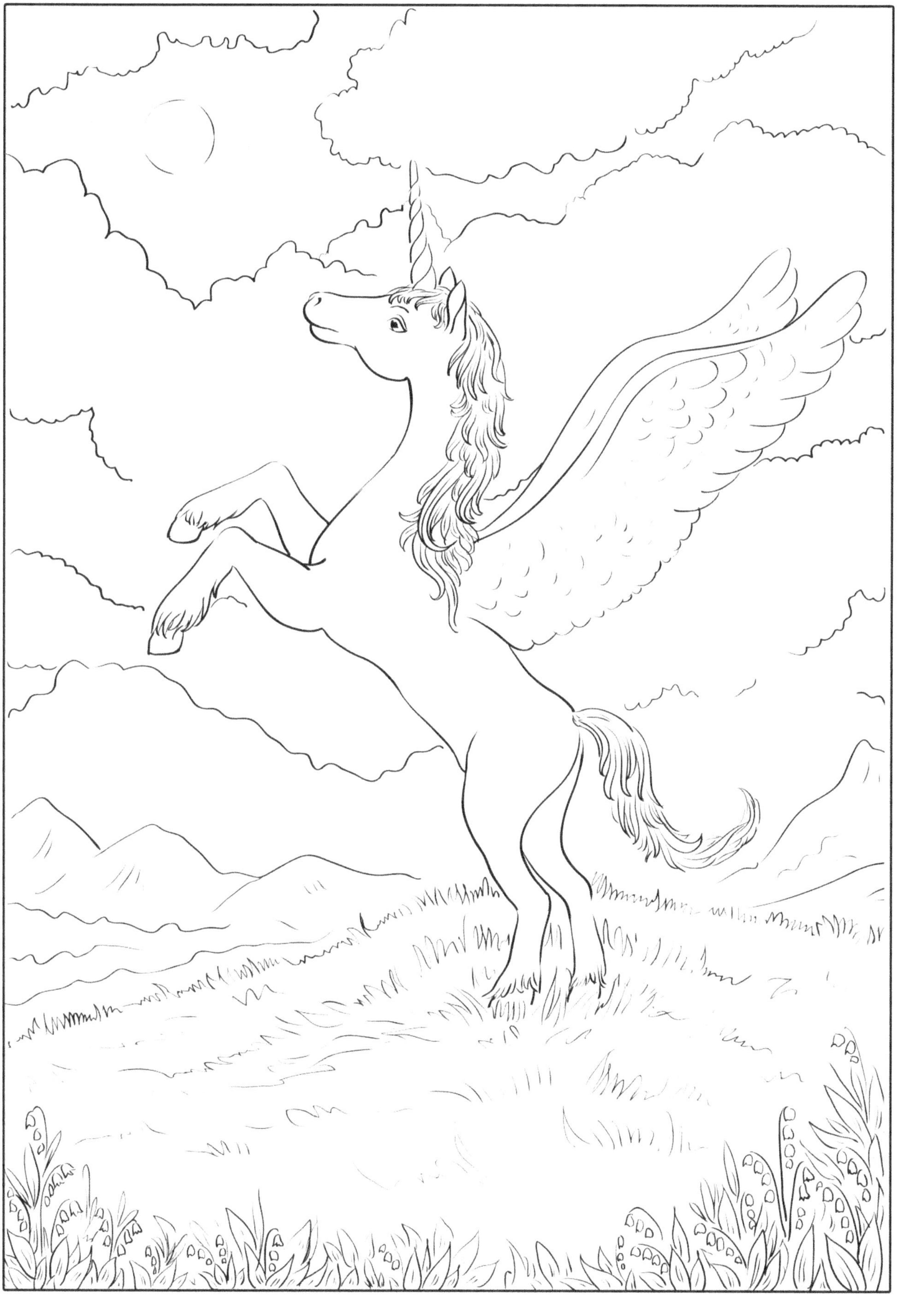

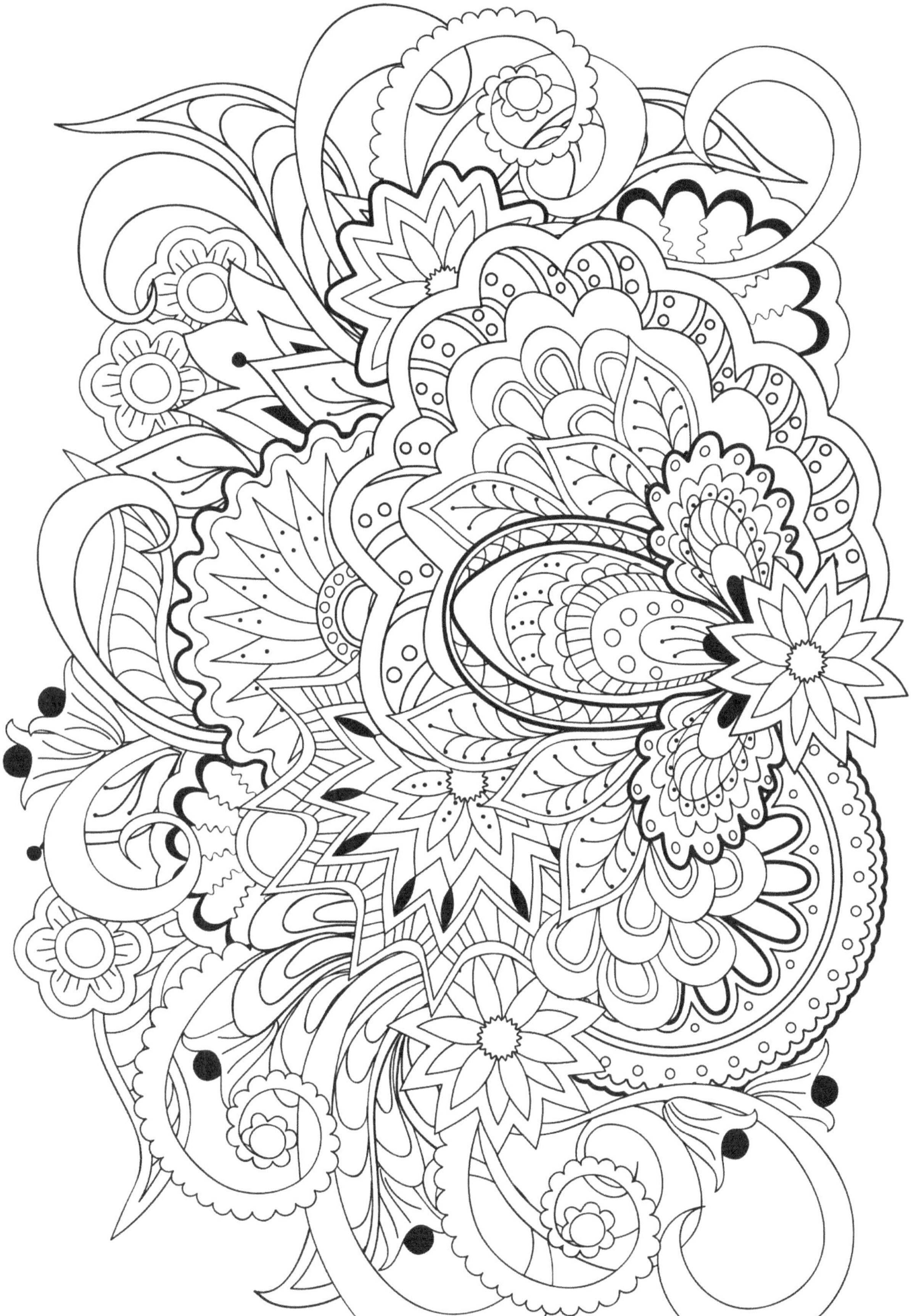

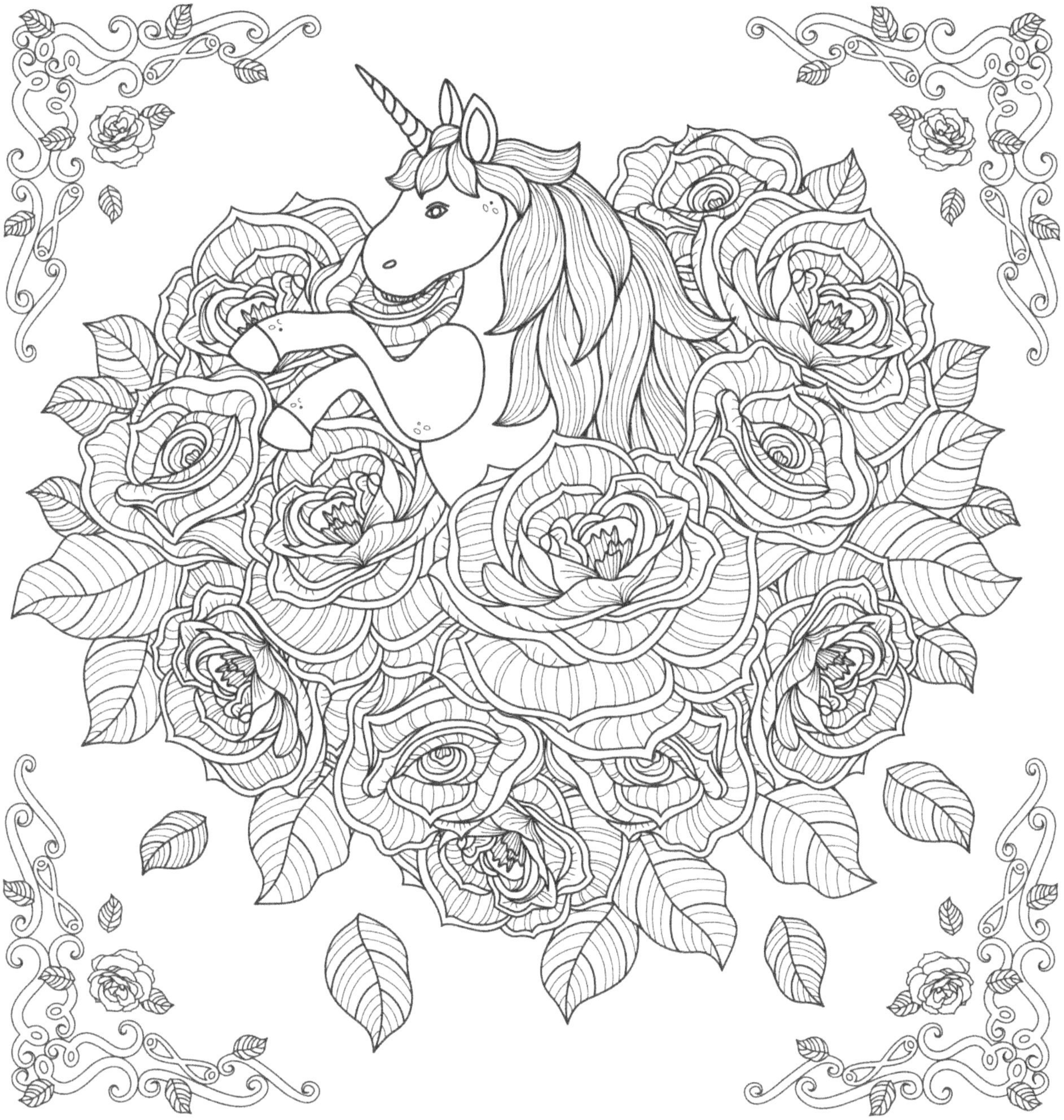

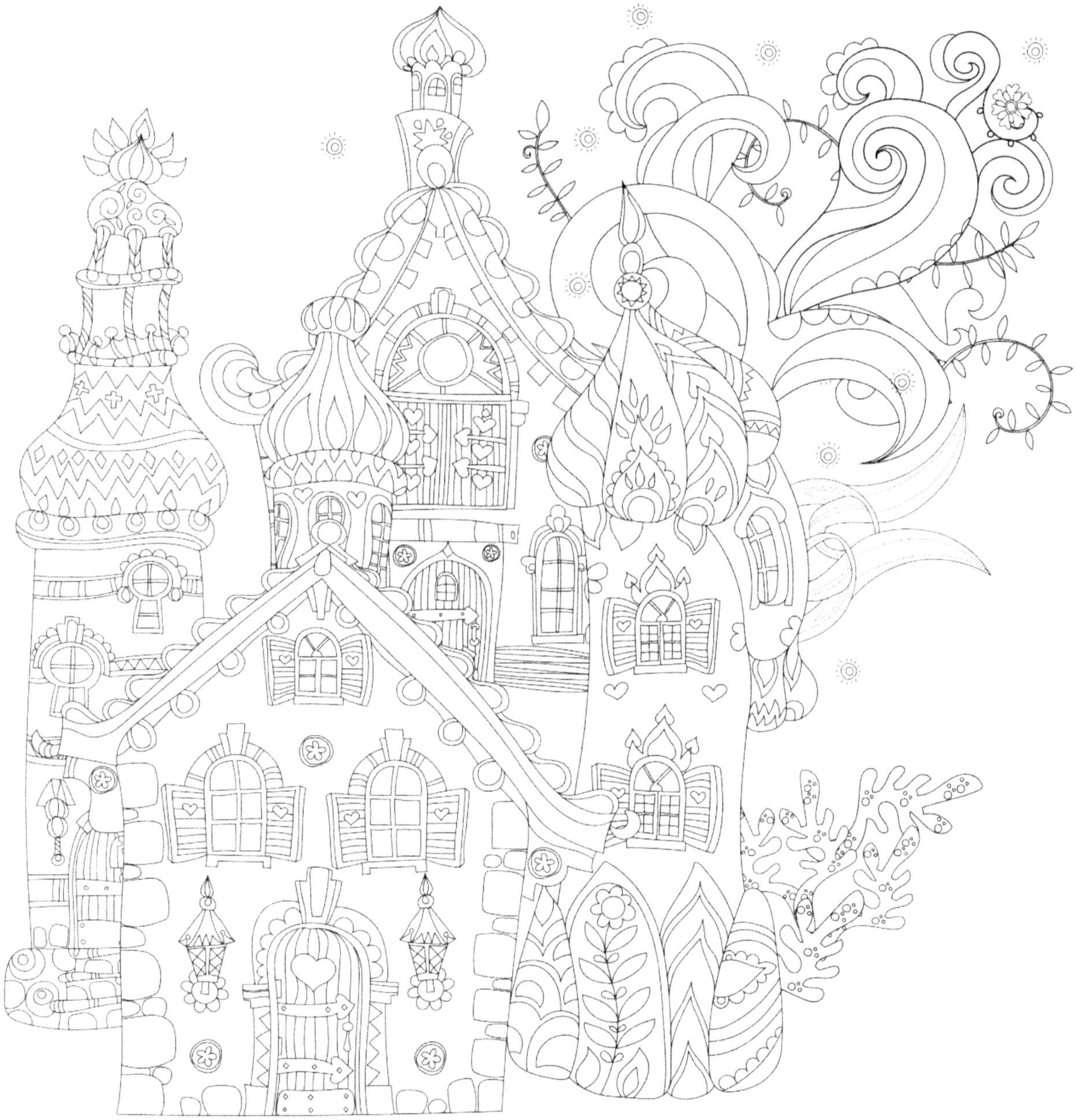

www.ingramcontent.com/pod-product-compliance
Lightning Source LLC
Chambersburg PA
CBHW081906170526
45167CB00007B/3169
* 9 7 8 1 5 4 2 9 3 7 1 6 0 *